# Art Masterpieces of
# THE LOUVRE

## Designed and Produced by
## TED SMART
## and
## DAVID GIBBON

## COOMBE BOOKS

# INTRODUCTION

The collection of art housed in the Louvre, one of the world's most impressive buildings, contains masterpieces from all periods and all cultures. The nucleus of the museum is, naturally, its national art, and it holds an incomparable collection of French masterpieces. Throughout the years, however, the collection has expanded to include paintings from all the great European schools and works of art from all over the world: the Louvre has avoided specialisation and obtained rare pieces from any period or country of origin. Today the Louvre offers the most comprehensive collection of art assembled under one roof anywhere in the world.

As its origin was the royal collection, the Louvre contains many rare masterpieces obtained by the Kings of France. It has been built up to the size it is today mainly by purchases of large collections and individual paintings, confiscated property from warfare, and the generosity of private benefactors.

The original building of the Louvre was a tower built by Philip Augustus in about 1190 in order to protect the west side of Paris. Under Philip, Paris became the residence of the crown. The building was used mainly as a fortress, but it housed the royal treasures and even at this early age Paris became a cultural centre, drawing artists from all over France, Italy and Flanders.

Until the reign of Charles V, who made major alterations, the building remained relatively unchanged. Many of the treasures within, however, were lost during the reign of his son, Charles VI, when the English conquered the French at Agincourt. The building subsequently lay neglected until the accession of Francis I who spent vast sums of money on its restoration, constructing a larger and far more elegant Louvre.

Francis I is considered the founder of the royal collection. During his military campaigns he developed an appreciation of Italian art and on his return he sought out the most precious works of art in Italy and gathered together some of the finest artists of the time. Many great artists including Leonardo da Vinci, who is believed to have died in the King's arms, shared his court, and at the time of his death Francis had accumulated many excellent works, including several pictures by Raphael, Leonardo da Vinci and Titian, establishing a great basis for the collection of masterpieces in the Louvre.

From the death of Francis I to the accession of Louis XIV, relatively little of importance was added to the royal collection. During the reign of Louis XIII some additions were made, including paintings by Veronese and Leonardo da Vinci, yet when Louis XIV ascended the throne, the whole collection amounted to little more than 200 pictures.

By commissions of artists, gifts and the purchase of many private collections, Louis XIV and Cardinal Mazarin built up the number to more than 2,000 with notable paintings by Raphael, Correggio and Titian. Many of the most important additions, including pictures by Giorgione, Caravaggio, Veronese, Titian and Holbein were obtained from the German banker Jabach, from whom Louis purchased over 100 paintings and 5,000 drawings, many of which had originally come from the famous collection of Charles I of England. Louis also acquired many French masters, notably paintings by Poussin, Claude Lorrain and his official painter Le Brun. In order to house the growing collection, Louis made substantial alterations to both the exterior and the interior of the building.

Except for works by Rembrandt, Rubens and Raphael, Louis XV added little, but a great contribution was made during the reign of Louis XVI. The Compte d'Angiviller was appointed to enlarge the collection, concentrating on filling the gaps, particularly in the French section, and make it accessible to the public.

The Louvre had been neglected since Louis XIV's departure to Versailles, and the idea of using the building as a public museum was presented by those concerned for the protection of such an important collection. Some of the masterpieces were exhibited in Luxembourg in 1749, creating the first public gallery, but it was only after the Revolution that the idea of a public museum came to fruition. In November 1793 the museum was inaugurated and from the proclamation of the Empire in 1804 the museum, known as Musée Napoleon, expanded rapidly with works of art plundered from conquered countries and confiscated from churches and fleeing aristocrats. It became the most stupendous gallery of all time and a respected institution. After 1815, however, 5,000 pictures were reclaimed and only about 100 of the 'plundered' masterpieces remain.

During the nineteenth century, extensions to the building were added to house the collection which was gradually expanding again. Several purchases were made including works by Géricault, Rembrandt, Memling and Murillo. During the reign of Napoleon III a considerable contribution was made with the purchase of the Campana collection and the La Caze bequest which is the finest donation ever received by the Louvre. Many important masterpieces were added and gaps filled, particularly of the French eighteenth century. With Paris at its height as the cultural centre of the world between 1890 and 1914, the Louvre benefited from many private donations which included amongst other excellent pieces of art, some Impressionist works.

Today the museum continues to be supported by numerous bequests and the Society of Friends of the Louvre. A purchase policy operates to expand the collection further. The French school is the best represented, with masterpieces by Claude Lorrain, Watteau, Delacroix and Poussin. From the Spanish school are works by Velázquez, El Greco, Ribera and Murillo and the German and Dutch schools are well represented with masterpieces by Rubens, Bosch, van Dyck and Dürer. The Louvre also holds about 300 Impressionist paintings and is regarded as the finest Impressionist gallery in the world. In the cabinet Rothschild, numerous prints and drawings may be seen by special application.

The wealth of treasures contained in the Louvre includes far more than paintings; within the building are separate sections of collections of Roman and Egyptian antiquities, Oriental art, sculpture, jewellery, furniture and a department of archeology of international importance. This book has chosen to concentrate on a selection of the Louvre's masterpieces of painting. Even if the other collections are not taken into account, it is evident that the Louvre is a meeting place of all races and cultures and all periods – a magnificent and comprehensive collection appropriately housed in a palace situated in the heart of the artistic capital of the world.

Leonardo da Vinci's famous masterpiece 'La Gioconda' ('The Mona Lisa') is shown *left*.

One of the best examples of the work of the Egyptian 'Old Kingdom' (2686–2160 BC) is the 'Seated Scribe' *left*. The statue is painted in red ochre and the eyes inlaid with iridal stones.

The enamelled brick panels of the 'Archers of the Persian King' *right* are from the palace of Artaxerxes II at Susa.

'Stela of the King Naram-Sin', *below* belonging to the Akkad Dynasty, is considered to be amongst the most beautiful creations of Mesopotamian art.

'The Code of Hammurabi' *below right* is a monumental block of black basalt depicting the seated Shamash the Sun god dictating the law to Hammurabi who was the most noted king of the Babylonian dynasty which rose to power during the first half to the second millenium.

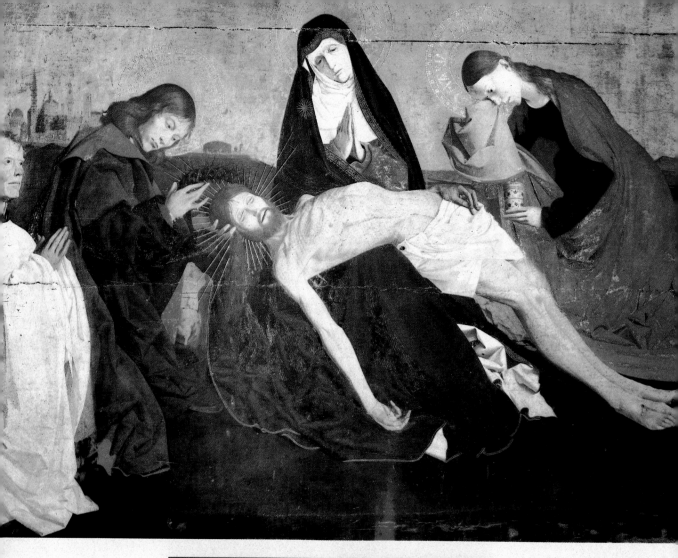

Originally in the Charterhouse of Villeneuve-les-Avignon, the 'Pietà' *above*, belonging to the School of Avignon of the mid-15th century, was saved from destruction by a parish priest in 1793 and it remained in the parish church until its removal to the Hospice in 1872. The panel was presented to the Museum, in 1905, by the Société des Amis du Louvre.

Jean **Clouet** (died 1541), who with son François, dominated French portraiture during the 16th century, was predominantly influenced by the Flemish School. His superb likeness of Francis I is shown *left*.

François **Clouet** (c. 1515-1572), who succeeded his father Jean as Court Painter, is also best known for his portrait painting. His work, however, differs from that of his father in that it shows links with Italian and German Mannerism; and his portrait of 'Elizabeth of Austria, Queen of France' pictured *right* is a fine example.

Jacques-Louis **David** (c. 1748–1825) was the foremost Neoclassical painter of his time and during the French Revolution became an ardent Bonapartist. Under the Republic he became the virtual Dictator of the Arts and the 'official artist' of the Revolutionary Government. Strongly influenced by classicism, David's aim was towards a simplicity of style, in the manner of Greek and Roman art which conveyed, within many of his works, the seriousness worthy of antiquity. 'Madame de Seriziat' *left* and 'The Sabines' *below* are two fine examples executed by David.

One of the outstanding portrait painters during the latter half of the reign of Louis XIV, Nicolas de **Largillière** (c. 1656–1746) was influenced by both Rembrandt and Rubens. A detail from 'The Artist and his Family' *right* is in the formal tradition and indicative of the style of Lely, for whom he worked as an assistant, during his time in England.

'The Betrothed in a Village' *above* is a perceptive study by Jean-Baptiste **Greuze** (c. 1725-1805), and the 'Tric-Trac Players' *below left* is the work of Mathieu **Le Nain** (c. 1607-77) and 'The Peasant Repast' *below right* by Louis **Le Nain** (c. 1593-1648). There has been, however, some confusion in the positive identification of individual paintings due to the fact that the three brothers appeared to have produced their work collectively under the name of 'Le Nain'. Louis is considered to be the most gifted and his portrayal of the gravity of peasant life is executed with sensitivity.

Maurice Quentin **de La Tour's** (c. 1704-1788) masterly pastel 'painting' of 'Madame de Pompadour' is shown *right*.

Jean-Antoine **Gros** (c. 1771-1835) was one of David's favourite pupils and, as a member of Napoleon's entourage, would have seen at close quarters many of the scenes which inspired his paintings. His masterpiece depicting 'Napoleon at Eylau' is shown *below*. Napoleon, wishing to commemorate the victory, made the battle the subject of a competition; but he wanted his humanity to be clearly shown in the painting, for, on the day following the battle, he had toured the field and, overcome by pity at the terrible sight before him, had uttered the words "If all the kings on earth could see this sight they would be less greedy for wars and conquests". Gros, urged to compete by Vivant-Denon, the Director of the Musée Napoléon, won the competition and received 16,000 francs for the picture.

Hyacinthe **Rigaud** (c. 1659-1743), the contemporary and rival of Largillière, painted copious portraits in an ostentatious and grandiose style depicting the sumptuousness of life at the court of the 'Sun King'. The official portrait of Louis XIV *right* shows the ostentation of the period with the king surrounded by all the accoutrements of royal dignity, including the sword that had once belonged to Charlemagne.

Jean Baptiste-Simeon **Chardin** (c. 1699-1779), the son of a Parisian cabinet-maker, was a painter who imbued his work with charm and delicacy.
Three lovely examples of his work are: 'Saying Grace' *right*, 'The Silver Goblet' *below*, and 'The Copper Fountain' *far right*.

The composition *above* by Anne-Louis **Girodet** Trioson (c. 1767-1824) was inspired by Chateaubriand's highly successful 'Atala' which was published in 1801.

The two panels *overleaf* 'Autumn' *left* and 'Spring' *right* are part of a series depicting the four seasons and were painted by the Milanese artist, Giuseppe **Arcimboldo** (c. 1527?-1593).

François **Boucher** (c. 1703-1770) was a gifted artist and an indefatigable worker. Although much of his work was flamboyant and sensual, by the use of mythological themes, he avoided coarseness, and the frivolity is firmly placed in a world of 'make-believe'.

'Vulcan's Forge' *above* was painted in 1757.

A noted decorative artist, having been appointed First Painter to the King under Louis XV, Boucher was also Director of the Gobelin tapestry works, designer for the Opera, and Madame de Pompadour's art master. His wide range of creativities also included engraving, (he succeeded in producing more than a hundred prints after Watteau,) whilst his series of 'Cris de Paris', depicting vendors and street criers of the city, is a noted example of his superb craftsmanship.

Two further paintings by this gifted artist are: 'L'Odalisque' *above*, and 'Renaud and Armide' *right*, which was painted in 1734 and was a reception piece at the Academy.

Jean Honoré **Fragonard**
(c. 1732–1806), the favourite
pupil of Boucher, was an
extremely talented artist who
used a wide variety of mediums:
oil, pastel, gouache and etching
to produce a plethora of 'œuvres'.
He also studied under Tiepolo
and the painting *left*, 'Women
Bathing' is believed to have
been painted before the artist's
first visit to Italy in 1756. The
French Revolution deprived
him of his patrons and after the
execution of Louis XVI and
Marie Antoinette, he retired to
his birthplace, Grasse, where he
died in poverty.
The rich variety of Fragonard's
paintings are beautifully
illustrated in 'La Chemise
Enlevée' ('The Chemise taken
off') *above* and 'Music' *right*.

'The Raft of the Méduse' *left* was
painted by Théodore **Géricault**
(c. 1791-1824) and based on a real-
life incident depicting the
survivors of the wrecked frigate,
the Méduse, at the moment of
sighting the rescue vessel, the
Argus.

'The Painter's Studio – A Real-life
Allegory', by Gustave **Courbet**
(c. 1819-1877) *below left* is typical of
Courbet's direct and realistic style.
Influenced by the philosopher
Pierre Proudhon, Courbet became
committed to Socialism and his
rejection of the romantic themes,
favoured by his contemporaries,
became even more apparent in his
later works.

'The Father's Curse' *below*, by
Jean-Baptiste **Greuze** (c. 1725-
1805), is one of a pair by this
talented artist who was greatly
admired by Diderot. 'The Broken
Pitcher' *right* is a particularly
charming example of his work,
although Greuze's sensitive
approach has often been criticized
for being over sentimental.

Claude **Lorrain** (Claude Gellée) (c. 1600-1682) was an outstanding landscape painter whose paintings were imbued with a nostalgic beauty so clearly discernible in the two examples of his work shown *above*, 'A Sea Port at Sunset', and *left*, 'Ulysses hands Chrysels over to her Father'. Claude spent most of his life in Rome and his gentle, ethereal art was subsequently to influence all future landscape painting.

The lovely portrait of 'Mlle. Rivière' *right* is the work of Jean-Auguste-Dominique **Ingres** (c. 1780-1867). Ingres was a true Classicist, constantly striving towards his ideal of purity of line, in keeping with the traditions of antiquity, and was greatly influenced by the work of Raphael, whom he fervantly admired.

**Ingres'** artistry is further exemplified by the beautiful works illustrated on these pages.

*Left:* 'The Turkish Bath'. Ingres formed the idea for this painting from the letters of Lady Mary Wortley Montague, who had described the interior of the harem baths which she had visited at Seraglio.

*Below:* 'The Great Odalisque'. Here Ingres has concentrated on perfecting his 'purity of line'.

*Near right:* 'La Source'. This painting, which the artist had started in Florence in 1820, was finally completed in Paris, in 1856.

*Far right:* the lovely portrait of 'Mme. de Sainte'.

*Below far right:* 'The Bather'. (The bathing woman, Valpinçon, which was executed in Rome, in 1808).

*Below right:* the portrait of 'Madame Rivière'.

Nicolas **Poussin**'s (c. 1594-1665) wide range of subject matter encompassed themes based on mythology, architecture, history and religion. His works are essentially those of an intellectual, with no hint of sentimentality and his strong use of colour shows the influence of Titian, for whom he had a great admiration. Poussin's greatness owes much to his sense of order and construction; he did not merely imitate the classic Italian and Greek themes of antiquity, but made his paintings living ideals founded on truth and heroism. He left his native Normandy as a youth, to go to Paris, where he remained until 1624, and it was during this period that he produced his series of Bacchanals. Once installed in Rome his initial influence was that of Caravaggio: however, after 1636 he studied Titian closely and his subsequent work was to reveal how extensively he was affected by his Italian connections. 'The Triumph of Flora' *right.*is a splendid example of his work.

'Dante and Virgil in Hell' *above* by Eugène **Delacroix** (c. 1798-1863) is considered to be the artist's first great composition and shows the influence of both Rubens and Michelangelo.


'The Lictors Bringing to Brutus the Bodies of his Sons' by Jacques-Louis **David** (c. 1748-1825) *right* portrays Brutus receiving the bodies of his sons whom he had condemned to death because of their traitorous actions. Executed during the time of the French Revolution, the painting was to have not only a profound political effect but also greatly influenced the French way of life. The classical Roman life-style was adopted by French society who sought to transform their homes and their fashions in imitation.

These further paintings by **Poussin** illustrate the artist's mastery and studied composition.

'The Inspiration of the Poet' *above left* is amongst the few paintings by Poussin presenting large figures.

'Orpheus and Eurydice' *left* is characteristic of Poussin's work during the time he was working in the Louvre. He has set the classic story in the Roman Campagna and depicts Orpheus serenading Eurydice on the riverbank.

'Diogenes and the cup' *above*, one of the first of the artist's landscapes, emphasises the lush, verdant background of the tranquil scene.

'The Shepherds of Arcadia' *right* shows a calm landscape with three shepherds and a shepherdess who are deciphering an inscription on the tomb around which they have gathered. The Latin inscription 'Et in Arcadia Ego', (Even in Arcady I am) reveals that death is ever present, even in the vales of Arcady.

'The Four Evangelists' *right*, the works of Jacob **Jordaens** (c. 1593-1678), is believed to have been painted between 1620 and 1625 and is considered to be among the best of Jordaens' work.
The painting is in excellent condition and the richness and quality of the varying degrees of impasto emphasise the physical presence of the figures.
The picture depicts John receiving divine inspiration for the writing of his gospel and although, on occasion, the subject matter was thought to be that of 'Christ among the Doctors', this theory has now been discounted.

The painting *above* by Théodore **Chassériau** (c. 1819-1856) portrays a scene in 'The Tepidarium' where the women of Pompeii would go to rest and dry after the bath.
It is a mature work by the artist, having been executed in 1853 and shows the influence of Ingres.

The two beautiful still-life paintings shown left are the work of Lubin(?) **Baugin** (c. 1612?-1663).
Baugin is considered to be the greatest French painter of this style in the 17th century, and
'Still life with Chessboard' *below left*, the most refined.
'Still Life with Pastries' *left* is another superb example of the artist's delicate work.

The mysterious yet poetic figure of 'Gilles' *above* is by the noted French artist, Jean-Antoine **Watteau** (c. 1684-1721), whose Rococo style and innovative 'fêtes galantes' paintings are amongst the most romantically inspired of the 18th century. He produced a large number of drawings, revealing his acute perception of human nature, which he used as a basis for his paintings. This sensitive artist died, at the age of thirty-seven, from tuberculosis.

Eugène **Delacroix** (c. 1798-1863), a revolutionary in the field of art, produced on canvas a rich variety of paintings of colour and imagination. His visit to North Africa, in 1832, inspired many of his works, some magnificent examples of which can be seen here.

*Left:* 'The Battle of Taillebourg' – sketch for the huge canvas which hangs in the Palace of Versailles.

*Right:*
'The Death of Sardanapalus.' At the palace of Ninevah the wives and animals of the monarch are being slaughtered before he too is led to his death at the stake.

*Below far left:* 'Tiger Hunt'.

*Below left:* 'Massacre of Scio'.

*Below:* 'Women of Algiers'.

'The Barricade' *right* by Ernest **Meissonnier** (c. 1815–1891) portrays an episode which occured during the 1848 revolution, which Meissonnier, as a captain in the artillery, witnessed. Seen from Mortellerie Street it shows the horror of the bombardment of the barricades around the Town Hall in Paris.

Honoré **Daumier** (c. 1810–1879), as a staunch republican, used his superb talent to portray, through the medium of art, his social comments on the times, and attacked the government for its corruption.

'The Washerwoman' *left* is one of Daumier's most powerful works and expresses the pathos and frugality of life for the working women of the era.

'Crispin and Scarpin' *below* evidences the artist's ability as a master of caricature.

'Port-en-Bessin, Outer Harbour, High Tide' *right* is the work of Georges **Seurat** (c. 1859-1891), a master of 'Pointillism' who fully developed this basically scientific technique with delicacy and precision.

Although Jean-Baptiste Camille **Corot's** (c. 1796-1875) art anticipates the Impressionist school, his roots lie basically in the Classical tradition. His early works were finely finished studio pieces, founded on conventional themes, yet at the same time he executed, in France and Italy, some beautiful paintings indicating his acute perception of the effects produced by the use of light and tone, and illustrated on these pages are some particularly fine examples.

'The Cathedral of Chartres' *left;* the fine figure portrait, 'Lady in Blue' *below;* and *below right* 'Woman with a Pearl'; a romantic work, the model's pose being similar to that of the 'Mona Lisa'.

Andrea **Mantegna** (c. 1431-1506), who worked almost exclusively in Northern Italy, was closely
associated with Padua, and for many years held the position of Court Painter to the Gonzaga family
at Mantua. He used the new art of perspective to convey solidity and reality to his scenes and
'Our Lady of Victory' *right* is an outstanding example of his work.

Born in Germany, Hans **Memling** (c. 1433-1494), became one of the greatest Netherlandish
painters of the 15th century, settling in Bruges in 1465, where he established his workshop. His
varied range of subject matter, for which he received many commissions, included portraits and
large-scale religious themes. 'The Resurrection of Christ' *above*, belonging to the artist's last period,
is the central panel of a triptych; the two outer panels portraying 'The Martyrdom of Saint
Sebastian' and 'The Ascension.'

REGINA
CELI LET
ALELVIA

(Domenico Zampieri)
**Il Domenichino** (c. 1581-1641),
famous for his charming and
simplistic frescoes in San Luigi
dei Francesi, Rome, was a pupil of
the Carrachi. 'Timocleus in front
of Alexander' *above,* painted with
clear and vivid colour is symbolic
of the new classical Idealism;
whilst 'St Cecilia' *right* clearly
shows the influence of Raphael.

The intricate composition
'Concert in Rome' *left* was painted
by Giovanni Paolo **Panini**
(c. 1692-1766). It illustrates the
performance which took place on
the 26th November 1729, to
celebrate the birth of the Dauphin
of France, first son of Louis XV.

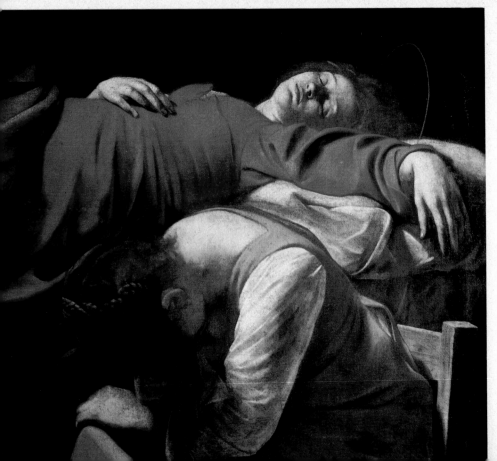

Antonio Allegri **Correggio** (c. 1499–1534) was considered to be the most advanced painter of his period and his masterly treatment of light and shade was to have an enormous effect on later generations. 'Antiope Asleep' *right* is one of two works on mythological subjects which he executed in 1521–22 before he commenced the decoration of the cupolas in San Giovanni Evangelista and the Parma Cathedral, and denotes the subtlety and sensuouness of his forms. His use of the smoky, atmospheric effect, known as sfumato, is indicative of the work of da Vinci.

Detail of 'Death of the Virgin' *left*, an outstanding painting by Michelangelo Merisi da **Caravaggio** (c. 1573–1619), shocked the ecclesiastics of the period who were outraged by what they considered to be the portrayal of the Virgin as a humble woman.

Illustrated *above*, 'View of the Salute Church in Venice', by Michele **Marieschi** (c. 1710–1743) was at one time thought to be the work of Canaletto.

Pietro Vanucci, known as **Perugino**, (c. 1446-1523) was the teacher of Raphael, and his gentle, dispassionate art is clearly discernible in the painting of 'Apollo and Marsyas' illustrated *above far left*.

'Massacre of the Triumvirate' *above* by Antoine **Caron** (c. 1527-1599) portrays, in a classical Roman setting, the inhumanities perpetrated in the name of religion.

The work of Paolo Caliari **Veronese**, (c. 1528-1588) 'The Nice Nani', *right* is a chatoyant painting typical of the Venetian school of the XVI century.

'The Wedding at Cana' *left* is one of **Veronese's** most successful works, with its iridescent colours and rich architecture. It was painted at the request of the Benedictine monks of San Giorgio Maggiore to decorate a refectory wall of the convent.

'Diana the Huntress' *above left* is of the School of Fontainebleau (c. 1550) and is believed to be an allegorical portrait of Diane de Poitiers, the mistress of Henry II of France.

One of the most renowned masters of the Italian Renaissance, **Titian,** (Tiziano Vecellio) (about 1477-1576) is recognised as an artist of outstanding ability whose work inspired some of the greatest painters in Europe.

His early training was in the Bellini workshop where he was decisively influenced by his association with Giorgione.

'The Entombment' *above* is one of his first religious compositions and shows clearly the dramatic content of the work.

'The Man with a Glove' *left* is believed to have been painted about 1522, and in this portrait Titian has avoided harsh, physical realism to reveal the sublime expression of the sitter.

The magnificent portrait *right,* 'Balthasar Castiglione', is the work of **Raphael** Santi (c. 1483–1520). This superb artist of the golden age of Roman High Renaissance, influenced by both da Vinci and Michelangelo, succeeded in obtaining the patronage of Pope Julius II.

This gifted painter, whose career began as assistant to the Perugino, moved first to Florence and then on to Rome. Here he was successful in training a large number of assistants who were able to continue his work after his untimely death at the age of 37.

**Leonardo da Vinci** (c. 1452-1519), an artist of genius and an outstanding draughtsman, was revered not only for his superb talents but also for his intellectual integrity. His mastery of sfumato, which imbued his paintings with a delicate mystery, is particulary apparent in the 'Mona Lisa', the most famous of all his paintings.
'Portrait of a Lady' *right* is believed to represent 'La Belle Ferronière', the daughter of a mastersmith and the last favourite of Francis I. 'St John the Baptist' *above*, a mystical painting with mellow tones, was found, on Leonardo's death, in his studio at the Château of Cloux.

The unusual theme of 'Virgin and Child with St Anne' *above left* has caused a certain amount of dissension in determining **Leonardo's** symbolic reasons for portraying the stream of life spanning three generations, yet the gentle, ethereal beauty shines as clearly as in the study of 'The Virgin of the Rocks' *above*. Two versions of this painting survive, the other being in the National Gallery, London.

The right-hand side of the panel, 'The Madonna of Chancellor Rolin', by Jan **van Eyck** (c. 1390–1441) is illustrated *right*. This exquisitely detailed picture has survived remarkably well, despite a certain amount of repainting and some premature surface cracking.

Commissioned by a wealthy spice merchant, Jacques Floreins, 'The Virgin of Jacques Floreins' shown *left* is the work of the Flemish artist, Hans **Memling** (c. 1433–1494).

Pieter **Bruegel** the Elder
(c. 1525-1569), considered to
be the foremost Netherlandish
artist of the 16th century,
painted uncompromising and
often harsh scenes of peasant
life. 'The Beggars' *above* is
typical of Bruegel's style and
approach, although it has
proved difficult to interpret
conclusively the meaning of
the work.

An outstanding Dutch still-
life painter, Jan Davidsz de
**Heem** (c. 1600-1688),
adopted, in his later work,
Baroque compositions using
lavish displays of exotic fruit.
A detail from one of his
superb paintings, entitled
'Still Life' is shown *left*.

The portrait of an 'old
Woman' *right* is by the
superlative portrait painter,
Frans **Hals** (c. 1580-1666),
whose forthright style was to
influence future Haarlem
artists.

The son of a wealthy Leyden miller, **Rembrandt** van Rijn (c. 1606-1669), went, in 1624, to Amsterdam, where he worked in the studio of Pieter Lastman, who introduced him to the art of the Italian Renaissance. Although Rembrandt, himself, never made the journey to Italy, his genius was recognised by his compatriots and he became a universally accepted master, noted for his superb ability to combine drama with the effects of chiaroscuro.
In 'The Pilgrims at Emmaus' *below* the impasto is used with moderation, and the amber shadows create a mystical atmosphere surrounding the central figure of Christ.

Albrecht **Dürer** (c. 1471-1528) was a painter and graphic artist whose intellectual foresight ranked him with the greatest of Italian masters. His innovations in portraiture; delightful watercolours of animals and plants, and his introduction of the nude figure to German art combined to establish his reputation as a man of genius which spread beyond his native country and was of particular consequence in the Netherlands. His self-portrait *left,* 'Portrait of the Artist', is believed to be a betrothal gift to his fiancée and shows the artist holding a sprig of 'Mannestrene', symbolising conjugal fidelity.

The dynamic qualities of one of the greatest of all European painters, Peter Paul **Rubens** (c.1577-1640), who made Antwerp an artistic centre, are clearly discernible in all the works of this highly gifted and remarkable man, who was the ideal artist of the Counter Reformation.

Illustrated on this page and overleaf are some magnificent examples of Ruben's distinctive artistry.

*Above:* 'The Education of Marie de Médicis'; *above right:* 'Village Fête'; *right:* 'The Coronation of Marie de Médicis at Saint-Denis'.

*Overleaf left:* 'The Capture of the Juliers', *overleaf right:* 'Hélène Fourment and her Children'.

*Page 64.* 'The Coronation of Napoleon', by Jacques Louis **David**.

First published in Great Britain 1979 by Colour Library International Ltd.
© Illustrations: Foto Scala, Florence, Italy.
Colour separations by La Cromolito, Milan, Italy.
Display and text filmsetting by Focus Photoset, London, England.
Printed in Spain by CAYFOSA
bound by EUROBINDER-Barcelona
ISBN 0 904681 86 6

Dep. Leg. B. 17.887/81